Christmas
Crafts

Christmas Crafts

A handy step-by-step guide

Sheherazade Goldsmith

LONDON, NEW YORK, MELBOURNE,
MUNICH, DELHI

Project Editor Katharine Goddard
Senior Art Editor Elaine Hewson
Managing Editor Penny Smith
Senior Managing Art Editor Marianne Markham
Producer, Pre-Production Rebecca Fallowfield
Senior Producer Katherine Whyte
Special Sales Creative Project Manager Alison Donovan

DK INDIA
Editors Janashree Singha, Manasvi Vohra
Senior Art Editor Balwant Singh
Art Editor Zaurin Thoidingjam
Assistant Art Editor Nikita Sodhi
DTP Designer Satish Chandra Gaur

First published in Great Britain in 2014
by Dorling Kindersley Limited
80 Strand, London WC2R 0RL

Material in this publication was previously published in:
The Christmas Book (2008)

A Penguin Random House Company

This edition produced for The Book People Ltd,
Hall Wood Avenue, Haydock, St Helens, WA11 9UL

ISBN 978-1-4093-6964-6

Printed and bound in China by Leo Paper Products Ltd.

Discover more at **www.dk.com/crafts**

Contents

Introduction

Christmas is a wonderful time of year that includes welcome yearly traditions: putting up the tree; carefully unwrapping the decorations; stringing lights around the windows and in the garden; and preparing a wonderful Christmas feast and tasty treats.

This Christmas, explore your creative side and make an assortment of tree decorations and handmade gifts for friends and family, or cook a selection of recipes for both savoury and sweet goodies.

None of the projects in this book require any particular expertise; most can be done without having to spend money on specialist tools or equipment, and all of them can be completed at home using everyday resources. A talented craftswoman has devised the projects, and each project has been tried and tested to ensure a great outcome.

To make sure you get the best results – get organized. It's a good idea to read through your chosen project thoroughly before you begin, then make sure you gather all the items together that you will need. Some projects can be messy, so it's advisable not to wear your best clothes but to cover up with an old shirt or overalls. The same applies to your work surfaces: use old newspapers or plastic sheeting to protect your table from damage.

Take your time, follow the instructions carefully, and before you know it you'll have created a wonderful collection of Christmas decorations, gifts, and edible produce. Most of the projects are simple enough for anyone to do, so have a go and enjoy the Christmas spirit.

Fabric garland

This charming garland is versatile enough to decorate mantlepieces, kitchen dressers, Christmas trees, and bedrooms. Store it carefully and it can be reused every year. You can make your own felt by washing an old cream-coloured, 100 per cent wool blanket or garment in a hot machine wash. You'll need brown felt for the gingerbread man.

materials

- Garland templates *(p.54)*
- Large piece of cream-coloured felt
- Brown felt for the gingerbread man
- Scissors
- Pins
- Eco-friendly marker pen
- Coloured embroidery thread (for blanket stitching and features) and needle
- Ricrac trimming
- 5 lengths of thin wire, each about 8cm (3in) long
- 1m (3ft) twine or string
- Pieces of recycled ribbon
- Old, unwanted woollen garment or scarf
- Recycled buttons

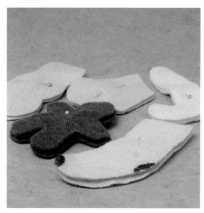

1 Cut and pin together two of each shape from cream felt, and two gingerbread men from brown felt. Decorate one stocking with the pen.

2 Sew the shapes together using blanket stitch. Leave mitten and stocking tops unsewn. Sew on facial features and details.

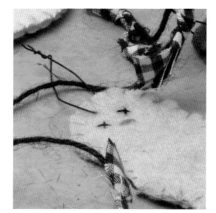

3 Thread a piece of wire through the top of each shape and secure in a loop. Thread the twine through the loops and tie ribbons onto the twine.

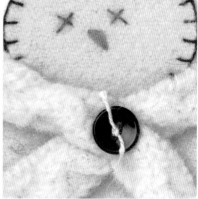

4 Cut strips from the garment for scarves and sew them, together with some decorative ribbons and buttons, onto the fabric shapes.

Cinnamon spice bundles

With its distinctly warm, aromatic smell, cinnamon spice can instantly create a familiar festive scent in any room. Golden-red cinnamon sticks, which are actually pieces of bark from the evergreen cinnamon tree, are easy to purchase and make striking natural decorations. Try sourcing long cinnamon sticks to make these spice bundles for your Christmas tree.

1 Secure the cinnamon sticks in a bundle with the elastic band. Thread the wire under the elastic band and secure it tightly in a loop.

2 Thread a nutmeg onto one end of the raffia. Tie a knot in the end of the raffia to secure the nutmeg. Repeat at the other end.

3 Wrap the raffia around the cinnamon bundle a couple of times so that the elastic band is completely hidden. Secure in a knot.

4 Glue the star anise onto the front of the orange slice, then glue the orange slice onto the raffia so that it covers the knot.

materials

For each decoration

- 6–8 cinnamon sticks
- 1 recycled elastic band
- Length of thin wire, approximately 15cm (6in) long
- 2 nutmegs with a hole drilled through the centre of each (use a clamp and fine-bore drill bit)
- Length of recycled natural raffia, about 50cm (20in) long
- Eco-friendly glue
- 1 star anise
- 1 dried orange slice

Make a peg doll tree angel

An old-fashioned peg doll has a nostalgic appeal that makes it a perfect decoration for any Christmas tree. If your tree is small, hang the angel right at the top of the tree, or for a larger tree make up several angels to dress the branches. Follow the steps below to create the angel's body and then personalize your angel with folded arms, facial features, hands, and a neck tie.

materials

- Recycled natural raffia
- 1 dolly peg
- Eco-friendly glue
- Eco-friendly marker pen
- Old tablecloth
- Templates (p.55)
- Scissors
- Cotton thread and needle, or sewing machine
- Garden wire, about 15cm (6in) long
- Cream felt
- Recycled ribbon

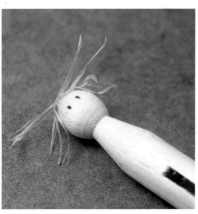

1 Attach a few short strands of raffia to the top of the dolly peg with a dab of glue. Draw two eyes onto the peg head with the marker pen.

2 Cut two shapes from the cloth using the template. Align and sew the sides of the dress together, leaving a gap in the neck to fit the peg.

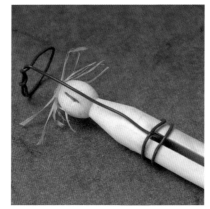

3 Twist one end of the wire into a circle. Bend the free end at right angles to the circle. Wind it around the peg to secure the halo in place.

4 Cut the wings from the felt using the template. Glue a loop of ribbon, then the dress, onto the wings. Glue the peg inside the dress.

Spiced orange decorations

Even after they have been dried thoroughly, oranges retain enough of an aroma to fill a room for many days with their citrus scent. Their mellow orange hues and cylindrical shape also mean that they make naturally attractive decorations, especially when hung from the vibrant green branches of a Christmas tree.

1 Glue the star anise onto the front of the orange slice, and the bay leaf onto the back. Secure a length of wire in a loop at the top of the orange.

2 Stick cloves into the clementine in a pattern. Push a skewer through the fruit, thread wire through the hole and secure one end in a loop.

3 Thread wire lengthways through the cinnamon stick. Bend one end over, thread the other end through the clementine loop, and secure.

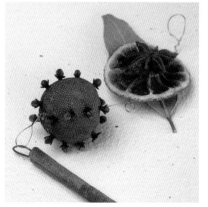

4 Attach the loose wire at the top of the clementine to the orange slice. The three parts should now all be joined together by wire.

materials

For each decoration

- Eco-friendly glue
- 1 star anise
- 1 dried orange slice
- 1 flat, dried bay leaf
- Several lengths of thin wire
- A handful of cloves
- 1 dried, whole clementine
- Skewer or knitting needle
- 1 cinnamon stick

 **Craft tip**

Dehydrating fruits
Arrange the sliced and whole fruits in a single layer on a piece of muslin on a wire rack. Leave to dry in a very low oven or a warm airing cupboard, which can take 48 hours or longer.

A flock of festive birds

These beautiful felt tree decorations are fun to make and last a lifetime. The basic method is straightforward; it's up to you how sophisticated you want the decorations and details to be. Take your inspiration from your favourite birds, and make them as colourful and vibrant as you like. So that they are uniquely personal, add a family member's initials to each finished decoration.

1 Cut two body and wing shapes and some flower and leaf shapes for each bird. Make a hole in the top of each body shape with a skewer.

2 Stitch a flower eye onto the outside of each body shape at the head, then sew some flower and leaf motifs onto the body and wings.

3 Embroider simple patterns onto the felt shapes, then sew the two body shapes together using blanket stitch. Repeat with the two wing shapes.

4 Cut a slit close to the top of the bird's body and push through the sewn wings. Thread the leather strip through the hole and tie it in a loop.

materials

- Felt in assorted colours
- Festive birds templates *(p.56)*
- Scissors
- Skewer
- Coloured embroidery thread and needle
- Leather strips or lengths of twine
- Found and recycled materials to decorate the bird (optional, see tip)

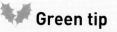 **Green tip**

Recycled decorations
Source a variety of items from the garden, or kitchen shelves, or drawers to decorate each bird. Look out for grasses, twigs, dried flowers, dried pulses, rice and pasta, bay leaves, old sweet wrappers, recycled buttons, and beads.

Scented fabric hearts

These pretty little filled fabric hearts look adorable hanging from a tree, but they can also be given as stocking fillers to be hung in wardrobes or tucked into drawers to fragrance clothes. Dried lavender flowers or natural pot pourri both make ideal fillings, or fill the hearts with grains of dried rice or barley fragranced with a few drops of your favourite scented essential oil.

1 Using the template, cut out two heart shapes from the fabric. Align and sew them together around the edges, leaving a small gap on one side.

2 Snip gently around the edges of the seams with the scissors, taking care not to cut the stitching. Then turn the fabric inside out.

3 Iron the fabric to get rid of any creases, then pack the heart with the scented filling. Sew up the open gap with the needle and thread.

4 Make a knot at one end of the string and sew it onto the heart. Thread the string through the stick and leaves, knot it, and finish in a loop.

materials

- Heart template *(p.58)*
- Recycled fabric (use an old gingham tea towel or tablecloth)
- Scissors or pinking shears
- Cotton thread and needle
- Your choice of filling, such as dried lavender
- Length of string
- 1 cinnamon stick with a hole through the centre (use a knitting needle or skewer to do this)
- Several dried bay leaves with a hole through the centre of each

Fabric candy cane cones

These cones look utterly irresistible when filled with sweet treats and hung from the tree. If you line the inside of each cone with a little baking parchment to protect the fabric from the sugary treats, you can use these decorations over and over again. For a more rustic effect, wrap the piece of wire around your finger and into a coil first, before attaching it to the cone.

materials

For each decoration

- A piece of cream felt (use an old felted blanket, *p.8*)
- Recycled fabric for lining
- Template *(p.59)*
- Scissors
- Pins
- Cotton thread and needle or sewing machine
- Knitting needle
- Coloured embroidery thread for sewing around the rim of the cone
- A short length of recycled ribbon
- Vintage or recycled button
- Red wool (optional)
- A length of wire approximately 50cm (20in) long

1 Cut one cone shape from the felt and one from the lining fabric. Align and pin the fabric shapes together, correct sides facing inwards.

2 Stitch the short edges together. Fold lengthways, correct sides facing inwards. Stitch the curved edges together, leaving the lining half unsewn.

3 Turn the fabric inside out through the gap in the lining using a knitting needle. Leave a band of lining showing at the top of the cone.

4 Sew around the rim to hold the lining in place. Decorate with a ribbon and button, or sew on red wool spots. Attach the wire at either side.

Evergreen centrepiece

A special seasonal foliage centrepiece will dress your table perfectly and set the scene for a festive meal. Evergreen foliage such as bay and conifer will last well and look fresher for longer than some other varieties, but choose whatever you have available in the garden, or can buy, to make the best-looking table display.

materials

- Deep, fluted flan tin
- 1 large candle
- Small bunches of evergreen foliage, such as bay and conifer
- Secateurs
- Thin garden wire
- A few pine cones

1 Place the flan tin on a flat, level surface. Use a tin with a fixed, rather than a removable, base, so that water won't leak out of it.

2 Position the candle in the centre of the tin. If you wish, you can stick the candle in place, but use a waterproof glue to do this.

3 Cut the conifer foliage into small bundles using secateurs. Tie wire around each bundle and place them in the tin around the candle.

4 Insert other foliage in between the conifer bundles. Position the pine cones around the candles and add a little water to keep the foliage fresh.

Advent calendar sacks

If you want a change from the traditional, flat card Advent calendars, try making these fabric sacks to hang on your Christmas tree, or use them to decorate a smaller table-top tree. They are easy to make, and can be filled with whatever treats your family enjoys – try a mixture of home-made sweets, bite-size cookies, fresh nuts, and tiny gifts.

1 Using the template, cut the cloth into 48 sack shapes. Then cut 24 small squares of fabric, each about 3 x 3cm (1¼ x 1¼in) in size.

2 Align two sack shapes, correct sides facing inwards. Sew three sides together. Leave a seam of 1cm (½in). Repeat with the other shapes.

materials

- Template (p.58)
- Old tablecloth, or pretty curtain material
- Scissors or pinking shears
- Cotton needle and thread, or sewing machine
- Eco-friendly marker pen
- 24 lengths of garden twine or string, each about 32cm (12½in) long
- Treats to fill each sack

3 Mark a day of Advent, from 1 to 24, on each fabric square. Make a hole in the top corner of each square, thread through the twine, and knot it.

4 Fill each sack with a few treats, then tie the twine around the top to seal the sack. Secure the ends in a loop and hang from the tree.

Recycled paper cards

These cards are easy to make, and are a fun, child-friendly project. Tear out pages from old magazines with interesting patterns, illustrations, and festive photographs, or recycle wrapping paper, wallpaper samples, or the pictures from last year's Christmas cards. Use a selection of templates from the back of the book to cut out different shapes, or download some from the internet.

materials

- Templates *(p.57)*
- Recycled pictures
- Scissors
- Plain, recycled card (or source ready-made, plain recycled cards)
- Scalpel
- Ruler
- Eco-friendly glue

🍃 Green tip

Recycle your old cards
Converting timber into paper is a very energy intensive process, but recycling conserves resources and saves energy. If all Christmas cards sent in the UK each year were recycled and not sent to landfill, around 248,000 trees would be saved.

1 Draw a template of your choice and cut it out. If you are using a star template from p.57, make up the smallest star template as well.

2 Place the template on a piece of illustrated or patterned recycled paper. Draw around the template and cut out the shape.

3 Lightly score down the middle of the recycled card with a scalpel and ruler. Fold the card in half and glue the star shape onto the front.

4 Using the smallest star template, cut tiny stars from the recycled paper and glue them onto the card around the main star. Allow to dry.

Glossy lip balm

This organic lip balm gives lips a pretty sheen, and its rich butters and oils nourish the skin and prevent drying: petrochemical-based balms actually dry lips out over time, whereas this balm soothes and gradually smooths away dryness. Package the lip balm in a pretty box lined with recycled tissue paper and tied with a vintage ribbon or some natural raffia.

1 Put the cocoa butter, coconut oil, almond oil, and beeswax in a heatproof bowl and melt them together in a bain marie.

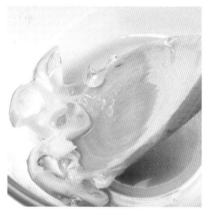

2 Remove from the heat. Add the gel and your choice of essential oil (peppermint is invigorating and zingy; orange is aromatic and delectable).

3 Mix the ingredients together using the whisk. The ingredients will cool quite quickly as you whisk, and turn an opaque colour.

4 Decant the mixture into the sterilized pot with a clean, dry teaspoon, and seal. Then package up the lip balm.

materials

- 1 tsp cocoa butter, grated
- ½ tsp coconut oil
- 1 tsp sweet almond oil
- ½ tsp beeswax
- 1 tsp aloe vera gel
- 2 drops sweet orange or peppermint essential oil
- 1 small whisk
- 1 small recycled eye cream or lip balm pot and lid, sterilized

Green tip

Use organic products
Not all chemicals are bad for us, but harsh industrial chemicals in non-organic face and body products are. Use organic products or read ingredients labels and avoid parabens, fragrance (parfum), and detergents such as sodium lauryl sulphate.

Relaxing bath oil

This simple organic bath oil recipe can be easily adapted to make a luxuriously soothing bath oil or an invigorating bath oil, just by changing the essential oils you use. Package the bottled oils in a recycled box lined with coloured tissue papers and include some of the ingredients for a rustic finish, or simply tie a length of beautiful vintage ribbon around the neck of each bottle.

materials

- 50ml (2fl oz) sweet almond oil
- 1 pretty recycled bottle and lid, sterilized
- 10 drops of sandalwood essential oil
- 5 drops of jasmine essential oil
- 5 drops of orange essential oil
- 1 label

For a Soothing bath oil
- 10 drops of rose essential oil
- 5 drops of chamomile essential oil
- 5 drops of lavender essential oil

For an Invigorating bath oil
- 10 drops of grapefruit essential oil
- 5 drops of lemon essential oil
- 5 drops of juniper essential oil

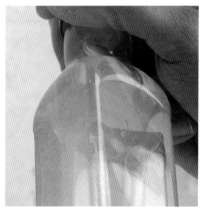

1 Carefully decant the almond oil from a measuring cup into the sterilized bottle.

2 Add each of the different essential oils, drop by drop, to the almond oil in the bottle.

3 Screw on the lid firmly and shake the bottle until the ingredients are well blended.

4 Attach a label identifying the oil, and with instructions to add 1 tablespoon of the oil to a warm bath.

Stocking Advent calendar

Add to the excitement of present-giving with this simple Advent calendar, which can be hung across a mantlepiece, along your stair banisters, or around a tree. Fill each stocking with a few of your family's favourite sweet treats, small edibles, or tiny gifts, attach fabric numbers to the stockings if you wish, and then mark the 24 days of Advent by opening each stocking in turn.

materials

- An old, plain linen bed sheet, or two plain linen pillowcases
- An old gingham tablecloth, or two large gingham tea towels
- Template (p.60)
- Scissors or pinking shears
- Pins
- Cotton thread and needle, or a sewing machine
- 24 short lengths of twine or string, each about 15cm (6in) long
- A long length of twine or string
- Fabric numbers (optional) (p.25)

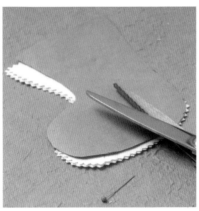

1 Cut 24 shapes from the linen cloth using the template (secure with a pin if necessary). Cut another 24 shapes from the gingham cloth.

2 Align two shapes of the same fabric. Sew the edges, but not the top, together, correct sides facing out. Repeat with all the fabric shapes.

3 Tie each short piece of string in a loop. Sew a loop onto the top right corner of each stocking. Sew on small bows made from the fabric.

4 Tie the stockings, alternating the fabrics, into place along the long length of twine so they are evenly spaced. Add fabric numbers if needed.

Sew a pair of felt slippers

These cosy home-made slippers make an ideal gift for a child, but find out his or her shoe size first so that the slippers will fit properly. The templates illustrated on pages 60–61 are based on a child's 11½ shoe size (European size 30), so enlarge or reduce the template accordingly. Use soft material, such as a shrunken woollen scarf, so that the slippers feel really comfortable.

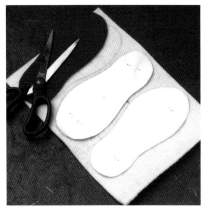

1 Cut out two left feet and two right feet from the thick white felt. Then cut out one left foot and one right foot from the red felt.

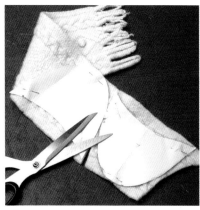

2 Cut one left and one right upper from the scarf using the other template. You should now have three cut-outs for each foot, and two uppers.

materials

- Templates (pp.60-61)
- Thick felt for the soles, in two different colours
- Shrunken woollen scarf or pieces of coloured felt for the uppers
- Pins
- Scissors
- White wool, coloured wool, and a large darning needle

3 Pin the right upper to one of the white right soles and sew the two pieces together at the edge with white wool using running stitch.

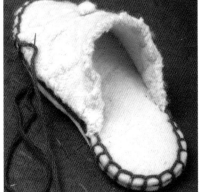

4 Align the three felt soles, pin them together, then sew together using coloured wool and blanket stitch. Repeat with the left slipper.

🦇 **Green tip**

Buy your gifts locally
If you don't have time to make many of your own gifts, buy them locally. Every year 4,000 tonnes of products are exported from China; if you shop in your local community, you'll support small suppliers and minimize your carbon footprint.

Recycled gift wrapping

Part of the pleasure of being given an imaginatively wrapped, beautifully presented gift is guessing just what might be underneath all the wrapping. If your gift is an unusual shape, put it in a discarded box first and then take the trouble to wrap the gift carefully so that the recycled materials you choose will look their best.

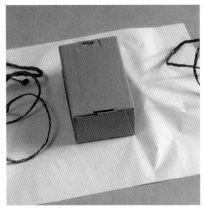

1 Put the gift in the box; shapes with flat, angular sides are easier to wrap neatly. Place the box in the centre of the paper.

2 Fold two sides of the paper over the box so they overlap. Wrap the string around the box and tie it in a knot to hold the folded paper in place.

3 Fold the paper carefully at each end of the box: press the paper neatly in towards the centre to create two triangular flaps at either end.

4 Fold down the flaps so they overlap. Wrap the string over the flaps to hold them in place, turn the box over, and secure the string in a bow.

materials

- Recycled cardboard box large enough to hold the gift (optional)
- Clean sheet of recycled paper, ironed on a low setting to get rid of creases
- Coloured string or ribbon (iron the ribbon on a low setting, or run through heated hair straighteners, to get rid of any creases)

🍂 Green tip

Avoid sticky tape
Paper can't be reused if it is covered in sticky tape, so use ribbon, upholstery trimmings, twine, raffia, wool, or string instead. Use paper-based, water-activated, gummed tape to post a gift; PVC tape has a negative

Bake walnut bread

To help bread cook well, mist the inside of the oven with a water spray just before baking the dough. The loaf is cooked if it sounds hollow when tapped on the base. This walnut bread will keep in the bread bin for up to four days, and it also freezes well. If you want to reheat it in a low oven, rub a little water over it beforehand to prevent it drying out as it warms up.

ingredients

Makes 2 ring loaves
Preheat the oven to 230°C (450°F/Gas 8)

- 400g (14oz) plain, white, strong bread flour
- 100g (3½oz) dark rye flour
- 1½ tsp dried yeast
- 2 tsp salt
- 320ml (12fl oz) tepid water
- 200g (7oz) walnuts, crushed

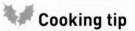 **Cooking tip**

Kneading bread
The action of kneading warms and stretches the gluten in flour. This elasticity, and the action of yeast, gives bread its light, springy texture. Press and stretch the dough away from you, then lift the edges into the middle, give it a quarter turn, and repeat.

1 Mix the flours together, then add the yeast and salt. Add a little of the water and mix the ingredients. Gradually add more water until the mixture becomes a dough.

2 Add the nuts to the dough, knead the dough for 5–8 minutes until pliable, place it in a lightly oiled bowl, cover with a damp tea towel, and leave it to rest until it doubles in size.

3 Turn the rested dough out onto a clean, lightly floured surface again and divide it into two equal amounts. Knead each half of the dough into a tight ball.

4 Shape each ball into a ring with a hole the size of a fist. Place on a lightly floured baking sheet and cover with a damp tea towel until they double in size. Then bake for 20–25 minutes.

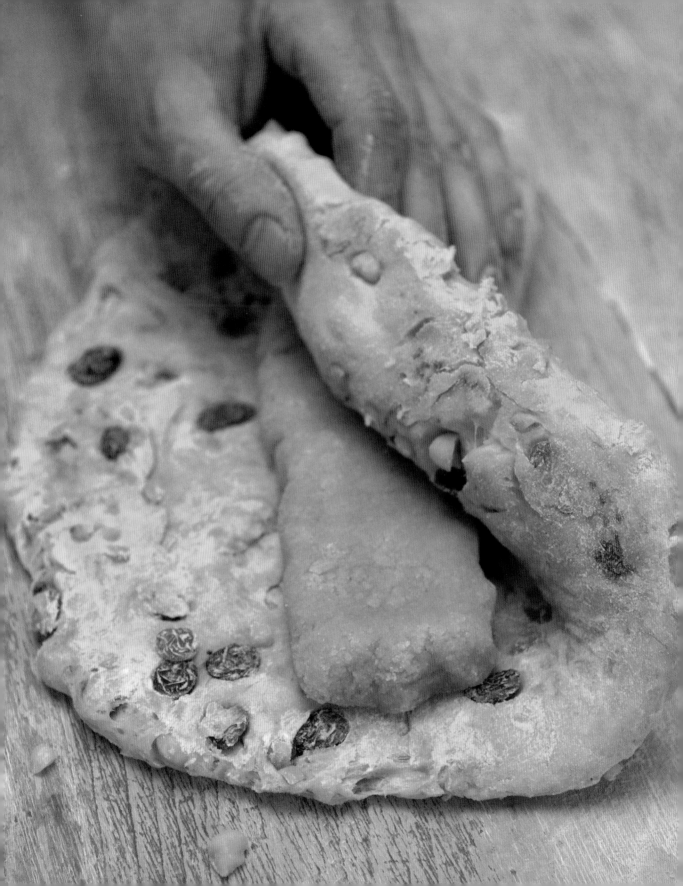

Stollen

This rich, German Christmas bread is filled with rum-soaked fruits and wrapped around an almond paste centre – symbolizing the baby Jesus wrapped in swaddling clothes. The loaf is baked if it sounds hollow when tapped on the base. As you let it cool on a wire rack, brush the top with melted butter, and then dust with icing sugar just before serving it. Stollen also freezes well.

1 Put the sultanas and currants in a small bowl. Warm the rum in a small pan, then pour it over the fruits and leave to one side to allow the alcohol to soak into the fruits.

2 Mix the flour, sugar, and spices, pour in the yeasty milk, and make a batter. Cover with a dry tea towel and leave in a warm place for half an hour. Then add the butter and egg.

3 Mix into a dough, knead for 8–10 minutes *(p.38)*, rest for 1–2 hours, or until doubled in size. Mix the filling ingredients into a paste. Knead all the fruits and nuts into the dough.

4 Roll the dough into an oval shape. Form the paste into a long roll, put it in the centre, fold the dough over the paste, brush the edges with milk, rest for 40–60 minutes, and bake.

ingredients

Preheat the oven to 200°C (400°F/Gas 6)

Bake for 30 minutes

- 75g (3oz) sultanas
- 50g (2oz) currants
- 3 tbsp rum
- 375g (13oz) plain, white, strong bread flour
- 50g (2oz) caster sugar
- ½ tsp ground cardamom
- 1½ tsp ground cinnamon
- 2 tsp dried yeast mixed with 170ml (6fl oz) lukewarm milk to give a creamy consistency
- 50g (2oz) butter, melted
- 1 egg, lightly beaten
- 50g (2oz) mixed chopped peel
- 50g (2oz) blanched whole almonds, chopped

For the almond filling
- 115g (4oz) ground almonds
- 50g (2oz) caster sugar
- 50g (2oz) icing sugar
- 1½ tsp lemon juice
- ½ egg, lightly beaten

Mini panettone

This sweet Italian Christmas bread is rich in butter, eggs, and dried fruits, yet it is deliciously light and soft. Italians traditionally have a slice of panettone with a glass of Champagne on Christmas day. Avoid leaving any dried fruit on the surface of the dough as you put it into the moulds, or it will burn in the oven and turn hard and bitter.

ingredients

Makes 12 mini loaves

Preheat the oven to 180°C (350°F/Gas 4)

Bake for 20 minutes

- 12 mini pudding moulds, greased
- 500g (18oz) unbleached white bread flour
- ½ tsp salt
- 1 tsp dried yeast
- 120ml (4fl oz) lukewarm milk
- 2 eggs
- 2 egg yolks
- 150g (5oz) butter, softened
- 75g (3oz) caster sugar
- 115g (4oz) mixed chopped peel
- 75g (3oz) raisins
- Melted butter, for brushing

1 Sift the flour into a bowl, add the salt, and make a well. Whisk the yeast, milk, and eggs together, pour into the well, mix in a little flour to make a batter, and rest for 30 minutes.

2 Add the egg yolks, softened butter, and sugar, and mix them and the rest of the flour into the batter with a fork. Then bind the ingredients together into a ball with your hands.

3 Knead the dough for 5 minutes (p.38) and leave to rest in a warm, but not too warm, place for 1½–2 hours, or until doubled in size. Then scatter over the peel and raisins.

4 Gently knead in the peel and the raisins. Divide into 12, place in the moulds, cover with a dry tea towel, and rest for 1 hour. Then brush the tops with melted butter and bake.

Vanilla cookies

The melted sweets in these cookies look like tiny stained-glass windows when they catch the light. Make a mixture of some plain cookies and some with sweet centres, and if you want to hang the biscuits from your tree as edible decorations, make a small hole in the top of each shape before baking them. The sweet mix is very hot as the cookies come out of the oven, so take care.

ingredients

Makes 12 cookies
Preheat the oven to 190°C
(375°F/Gas 5)

- 100g (4oz) butter
- 275g (10oz) caster sugar
- ½ tsp vanilla extract
- 2 eggs
- 525g (18oz) plain flour
- 2 tsp baking powder
- 2 tsp ground cinnamon
- ½ tsp salt
- A little milk
- A handful of hard-boiled organic sweets, crushed (put sweets of one colour in a clean, recycled plastic bag and crush them with a rolling pin)

1 Place buttered greaseproof paper over two large baking trays. Cream together the butter and sugar in a large bowl. Add the vanilla extract and stir in the eggs.

2 Sift the flour, baking powder, cinnamon, and salt into a separate bowl. Add the egg mix and then the milk, a little at a time, and mix into a dough. Chill for 30 minutes.

3 Roll out the dough on a lightly floured surface until 5mm (¼in) thick. Cut shapes using a large and small cutter. Transfer to the lined baking trays and fill each with a few crushed sweets.

4 Bake for 10 minutes. Leave the baked cookies on the paper and transfer the paper onto a wire rack. Allow the cookies to cool completely before removing them from the paper.

Chocolate brownies

Once packaged in an airtight tin, these irresistable chocolate brownies will stay at their best for up to six days. Don't overcook them or they will lose their soft, fudgy quality; look for a dull crust to form, then quickly take them out of the oven. You can make the brownies in advance, freeze them, and leave them to thaw in a tin – there will be no excess moisture.

ingredients

Preheat the oven to 190°C (375°F/Gas 5)

- 350g (12oz) plain chocolate, broken into small pieces
- 225g (8oz) butter, cut into small cubes
- 2 tsp instant coffee granules
- 2 tbsp hot water
- 4 eggs
- 225g (8oz) caster sugar
- 1 tsp vanilla extract
- 75g (3oz) self-raising flour
- 225g (8oz) plain chocolate chips or small chunks of plain chocolate

1 Grease and line a 30 x 23cm (12 x 9in) brownie tin with greaseproof paper. Put the chocolate pieces and butter in a small bowl.

2 Melt the chocolate and butter slowly in a bain marie: rest the bowl over a pan of gently simmering water on a low heat.

3 Dissolve the coffee granules in the water in a large bowl. Beat in the eggs, sugar, and vanilla extract. Then beat in the chocolate mixture.

4 Fold in the flour and chocolate chips. Pour the mix into the tin. Bake for 20–25 minutes, or until firm. Cool on a wire rack and cut into squares.

Sachertorte

This classic Viennese dark chocolate cake is one of the world's most renowned grown-up cakes. It's quite dense and rich, and not overly sweet, so ideally it should be served in small slices with a little unsweetened whipped cream on the side, accompanied by a cup of coffee or tea. The sachertorte will improve in flavour if you make it a day or so before you want to eat it.

1 Grease and line a round cake tin. Beat the butter in a large bowl or mixer until it is really soft. Meanwhile, melt the chocolate in a bain marie (p.46).

2 Add the sugar to the butter and beat until the mixture is light and fluffy. Add the vanilla extract and mix well. In a separate bowl, whisk the egg whites until stiff.

3 Add the melted chocolate to the mix, then the egg yolks, one at a time, and the ground almonds and flour. Add about one third of the egg whites and stir well.

4 Fold in the remaining egg whites, pour into the tin, and bake. Once the cake is cool, brush the jam thinly over the surface, spread the chocolate and cream mix on top, and chill.

ingredients

Preheat the oven to 180°C (350°F/Gas 4)

Bake for 35 minutes

- 150g (5oz) unsalted butter, softened
- 150g (5oz) plain chocolate, broken into pieces
- 100g (4oz) caster sugar
- ½ tsp vanilla extract
- 5 large eggs, separated, with the whites put into a large bowl
- 75g (3oz) ground almonds
- 40g (1½oz) plain flour

For the topping
- 4 tbsp apricot jam, melted
- 150g (5oz) plain chocolate, melted in a bain marie and then mixed with 200ml (7fl oz) double cream

Marshmallow sweets

It's essential that you use a sugar thermometer to achieve the correct boiling point when heating the sugar solution in this recipe. The sugar syrup is extremely dangerous at this high temperature, so take care and keep children well away from the pan. The soft marshmallows keep well for three to four days if stored in an airtight tin lined with baking parchment.

ingredients

- 2 tbsp icing sugar
- 2 tbsp cornflour
- 25g (1oz) gelatine powder
- 125ml (4fl oz) hot water
- 2–3 drops organic food colouring (optional)
- 500g (1lb 1½oz) granulated sugar
- 250ml (9fl oz) cold water
- 2 egg whites

🌿 Cooking tip

Toasting marshmallows
If children want to toast their marshmallows over an open fire, tie a fork handle securely to one end of a bamboo stick with a piece of string. Push a square of marshmallow onto the prongs of the fork and give the other end of the bamboo stick to the child to hold.

1 Lightly oil a cake tin. Mix the icing sugar and cornflour and sift a little into the tin to coat it. Dissolve the gelatine in the water in a small bowl. Add the food colouring.

2 Put the sugar and water in a large pan, stand a thermometer in the pan and heat the sugar syrup to 122°C (252°F). In the meantime, whisk the egg whites until stiff.

3 Take the boiling syrup off the heat and mix in the dissolved gelatine. Then gradually beat the syrup into the beaten egg whites. The texture should be thick and creamy.

4 Pour the mix into the tin and leave to set in a cool place. Once cool, cut into squares. Lightly coat each square in the icing sugar and cornflour mix. Store in an airtight tin.

Iced biscuit decorations

This simple gingerbread recipe is easy to follow and makes about 35 edible tree decorations. The dough is easy to handle, so children will love rolling it, cutting out different festive shapes, and decorating the baked biscuits with icing. Keep an eye on the biscuits while they bake, as they may burn.

1 Put the flour, bicarbonate of soda, ginger, and cinnamon in a bowl. Rub in the butter so the mix resembles breadcrumbs. Stir in the sugar.

2 Add the egg and syrup, then mix to form a dough. Turn out onto a lightly floured surface and knead to bring the dough together *(p.38)*.

3 Divide the dough into two batches. Roll each batch out with a lightly floured rolling pin to an even thickness of about 5mm (¼in).

4 Cut shapes with biscuit cutters, make a hole in each with a skewer, place on greased baking trays, and bake for about 10 minutes.

ingredients

Preheat the oven to 190°C (375°F/Gas 5)

- 350g (12oz) plain flour
- 1 tsp bicarbonate of soda
- 2 tsp ground ginger
- 2 tsp ground cinnamon
- 100g (4oz) butter, cut into pieces
- 175g (6oz) light muscovado sugar
- 1 egg, beaten
- 4 tbsp golden syrup

For the icing
- 1 egg white, beaten with 150–200g (5–7oz) icing sugar (adjust the quantity slightly, depending on the size of the egg; the icing should be smooth)

Fabric garland

See pages 8–9. Make templates of the shapes that you like and cut out two of each shape.

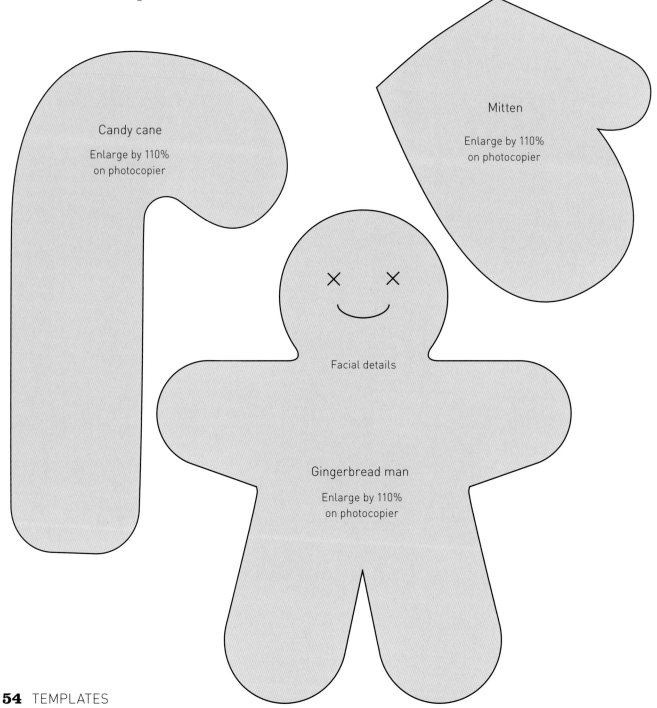

Candy cane
Enlarge by 110% on photocopier

Mitten
Enlarge by 110% on photocopier

Facial details

Gingerbread man
Enlarge by 110% on photocopier

Peg doll tree angel

See pages 12–13. Cut out two angel dress shapes in fabric and one wing shape in felt from the templates.

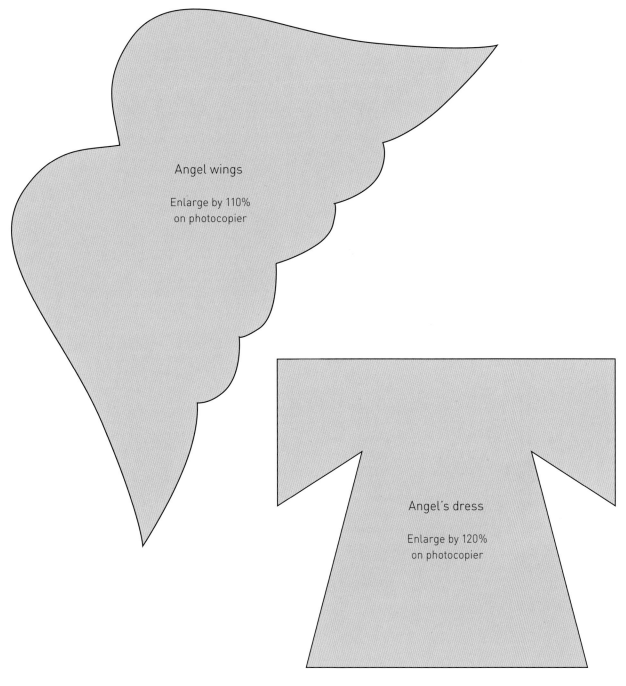

Angel wings

Enlarge by 110%
on photocopier

Angel's dress

Enlarge by 120%
on photocopier

Festive birds

See pages 16-17. For each bird, cut out two body shapes, two wing shapes, and several flowers and leaves from the templates.

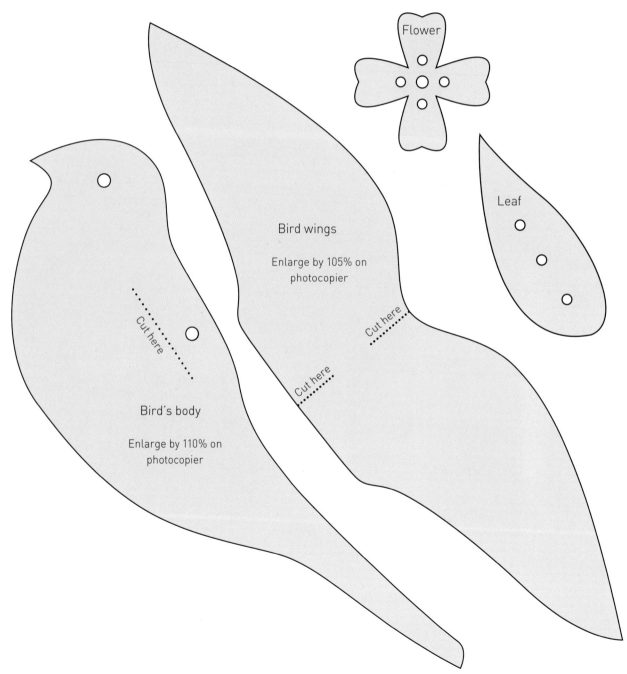

Flower

Bird wings

Enlarge by 105% on photocopier

Cut here

Cut here

Leaf

Cut here

Bird's body

Enlarge by 110% on photocopier

Paper cards

See pages 26-27.

Scented fabric hearts

See pages 18-19. For each fabric heart, cut two shapes from the template.

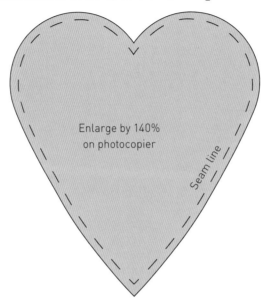

Enlarge by 140%
on photocopier

Seam line

Advent calendar sacks

See pages 24-25. For each sack, cut out two shapes from the template.

Enlarge by 130%
on photocopier

Seam line

Candy cane cones

See pages 20-21. For each cone, cut out one felt shape and one fabric shape from the template.

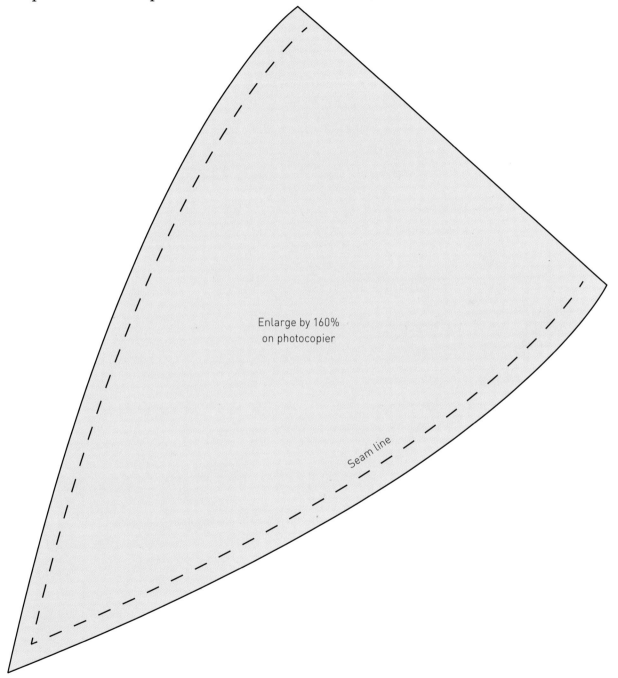

Enlarge by 160%
on photocopier

Seam line

Stocking Advent calendar

See pages 32-33. For each stocking, cut out two shapes from the template.

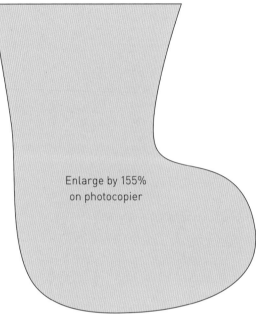

Enlarge by 155%
on photocopier

Felt slippers

See pages 34-35. Adjust the template sizes according to the foot size you want to make. Cut out one shape from each of the upper templates, and three shapes from each of the foot templates.

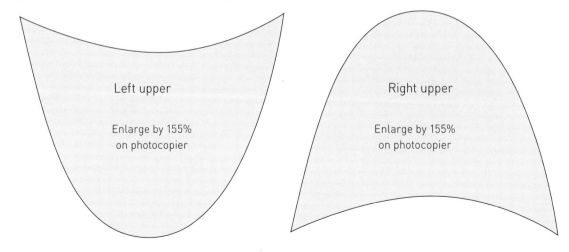

Left upper

Enlarge by 155%
on photocopier

Right upper

Enlarge by 155%
on photocopier

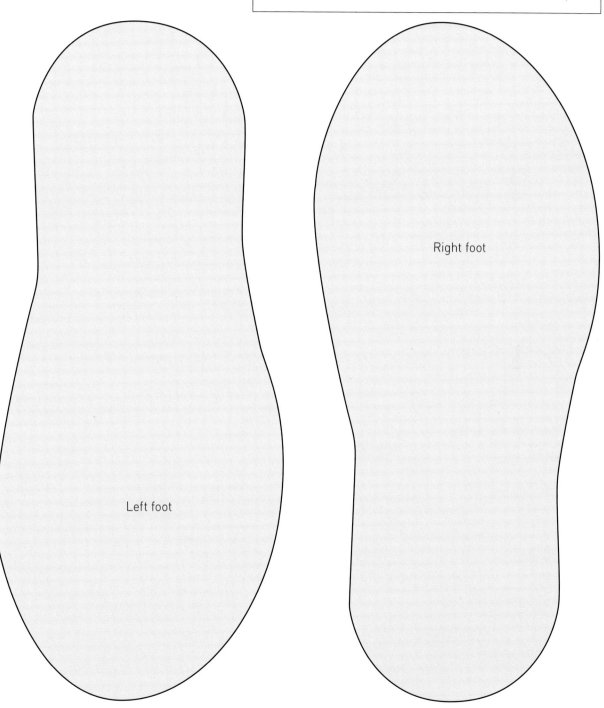

NOTE
These templates are printed at 100% of their correct size.
You may photocopy the templates for your own personal use,
or simply trace over the originals and cut around the shapes.

Right foot

Left foot

Index

Acknowledgments

Sheherazade Goldsmith would like to thank: Susannah Steel for writing the book and agreeing with all my ideas and edits. Jo Fairley for her workable beauty recipes. Ted & Harry for the prettiest recycled fabric decorations I have ever seen, and all the crafts people; Barbara Coupe, Francine Raymond, Lucy Harrington, Isabel de Cordova, Made in Hastings, Sparrowkids, and Caroline Zoob. Richard Scott for his delicious recipes and Kirsty Trotter for her endless patience. Peter Anderson for his beautiful photographs and everyone at DK. Lastly, my kids for making Christmas so much fun.

DK would like to thank all the crafters who created the projects that appear in this book, Valerie Lane-Glover and Pammie Riggs for valuable advice, Mike Wells, Jane at Not Just Food Ltd for testing the recipes, Ria Holland for design assistance, Helena Caldon for proofreading, and Marie Lorimer for indexing.